April 2012

U.S. POSTAL SERVICE

Challenges Related to Restructuring the Postal Service's Retail Network

GAO

Accountability ★ Integrity ★ Reliability

GAO-12-433

U.S. POSTAL SERVICE

Challenges Related to Restructuring the Postal Service's Retail Network

GAO
Accountability * Integrity * Reliability

Highlights

Highlights of GAO-12-433, a report to congressional requesters

Why GAO Did This Study

Since 2006, USPS has accumulated losses of $25 billion and projects a $14.1 billion net loss for fiscal year 2012. In September 2011, the Postmaster General testified that USPS needed to reduce its annual costs by $20 billion, or 27 percent of its projected expenses. One effort to reduce costs includes restructuring, or optimizing, the size of USPS's retail network and workforce. The network includes approximately 32,000 USPS-operated facilities, such as traditional post offices, as well as alternative non-USPS-operated locations that sell its products and services. To optimize this network, USPS plans to evaluate and locate its retail facilities to maximize revenue and minimize costs while still providing access to services.

As requested, this report discusses (1) key actions USPS has taken over the past 5 years to restructure its retail network, (2) concerns raised by stakeholders, and (3) the challenges USPS faces in changing its retail network. GAO analyzed USPS documents, interviewed USPS officials and stakeholders, and observed public meetings on retail facility closures.

What GAO Recommends

GAO makes no recommendations in this report, as it has previously reported on the urgency for Congress to allow USPS to adapt its retail network to changing customer behavior and reduce costs. USPS agreed with GAO's draft report, noting limitations it faces to retail restructuring. It also observed that maintaining the same level of retail services will require solutions to cover the costs of those services.

View GAO-12-433. For more information, contact Lorelei St. James at (202) 512-2834 or stjamesl@gao.gov.

What GAO Found

Over the past 5 years, the U.S. Postal Service (USPS) has taken several actions to restructure its retail network through reducing its workforce and its footprint while expanding retail alternatives. USPS officials estimated that it had saved about $800 million from reducing the number of work hours dedicated to retail operations. USPS also closed 631 of its post offices, but it did not have cost-savings estimates for these closures. Most of the facilities closed (500) were in response to a postmaster vacancy or the suspension of operations due to an expired lease or irreparable damage following a natural disaster. Fewer closures (131) have resulted from nationwide reviews that USPS initiated in 2009 and 2011. USPS has also restructured its retail network by expanding alternatives through self-service options as well as partnerships with other retailers.

Members of Congress, the Postal Regulatory Commission (PRC), the USPS Office of Inspector General (OIG), customers, employee associations, and some community residents have raised concerns about USPS's retail restructuring initiatives. The concerns include

- access to postal services, including community residents' ability to obtain retail services, the adequacy of retail alternatives, and changes to delivery services;
- the impact of facility closures on communities;
- the adequacy of USPS analysis of facilities facing closure and the reliability of USPS data, particularly the accuracy of USPS cost savings estimates;
- the transparency and equity of USPS closure decisions;
- the fairness of USPS's facility closure procedures; and
- changes in who can manage a post office.

PRC, USPS OIG, and GAO have recommended improvements to address some of these issues. In particular, GAO has recommended that USPS develop a plan that addresses both traditional post offices and retail alternatives and ensures that USPS has a viable strategy for effectively adapting its networks to changing mail use and maintaining adequate service as it reduces costs. USPS officials have said they are in the process of addressing these recommendations.

USPS faces challenges, such as legal restrictions and resistance from some Members of Congress and the public, that have limited its ability to change its retail network. For example, USPS is supposed to be self-financing, but it is also restricted by law from making decisions that businesses would commonly make, such as closing unprofitable units. Additionally, some Members of Congress and the public have challenged USPS's plans to close retail facilities in their districts or communities. Certain policy issues remain unresolved related to what level of retail services USPS should provide, how the cost of these services should be paid, and how USPS should optimize its retail network. Pending legislation takes differing approaches to addressing these policy issues. If Congress prefers to retain the current level of retail service and associated network, decisions will need to be made about how USPS will pay for these services, including through additional cost reductions or revenue sources.

Contents

Abbreviations

2009 Retail Initiative	Station and Branch Optimization Initiative
2011 Retail Initiative	Retail Access Optimization Initiative
OIG	USPS Office of Inspector General
PRC	Postal Regulatory Commission
USPS	U.S. Postal Service

United States Government Accountability Office
Washington, DC 20548

April 17, 2012

The Honorable Thomas R. Carper
Chairman
Subcommittee on Federal Financial Management,
   Government Information, Federal Services,
   and International Security,
Committee on Homeland Security and Governmental Affairs
United States Senate

The Honorable Darrell Issa
Chairman
Committee on Oversight and Government Reform
House of Representatives

Congress conceived of the U.S. Postal Service (USPS) as a financially self-sufficient entity that was expected to cover its expenses almost entirely through postal revenues,[1] yet at the end of fiscal year 2011, it had incurred a $5.1 billion loss for the year, had $2 billion remaining on its $15 billion borrowing limit,[2] and had not yet made its $5.5 billion scheduled retiree health benefits payment to the federal government.[3] Approximately 80 percent of its retail facilities do not generate sufficient revenue to cover their costs. Moreover, the number of USPS-operated retail facilities,[4] about 32,000, has remained largely unchanged over the past 5 years

---

[1] According to the Postal Reorganization Act of 1970, "[p]ostal rates and fees shall provide sufficient revenue so that the total estimated income and appropriations to the Postal Service will equal as nearly as practicable total estimated costs of the Postal Service." Pub. L. No. 91-375, 84 Stat. 760 (Aug. 12, 1970) (formerly U.S.C. 39 § 3621). *See also, Payments on Unfunded Liability by the U.S. Postal Service to Civil Service Retirement Fund: Hearing Before the Committee on Post Office and Civil Service, United States Senate, on H.R. 29,* 93rd Cong. 73-74 (statement by Post Office and Civil Service Committee Chairman Gale McGee).

[2] USPS is authorized to borrow $3 billion annually and a maximum of $15 billion. 39 U.S.C. § 2005(a). USPS borrows money from the U.S. Treasury via the Federal Financing Bank.

[3] Originally due at the end of fiscal year 2011, USPS's $5.5 billion retiree health benefit payment was delayed until August 1, 2012. Pub. L. No. 112-74 (Dec. 23, 2011).

[4] USPS-operated retail facilities include (1) main post offices, where local postmasters oversee retail operations in the geographic area; (2) postal stations located within a municipality's corporate limits; and (3) postal branches located outside a municipality's corporate limits.

                             GAO-12-433 U.S. Postal Service

even as visits to, and transactions at, postal retail facilities have decreased by about 16 percent and 18 percent, respectively. Also during this period, mail volume has declined by about 21 percent, and USPS's financial condition continued to deteriorate as net losses accumulated to more than $25 billion. USPS projects a $14.1 billion net loss for fiscal year 2012 and faces a continuing decline in the demand for its products and services. Figure 1 compares the decline in transactions and visits to USPS-operated facilities with the percentage decline in USPS-operated facilities over the past 5 years.

Figure 1: Percent Changes in USPS-Operated Retail Facilities, Transactions, and Customer Visits, Fiscal Years 2007-2011

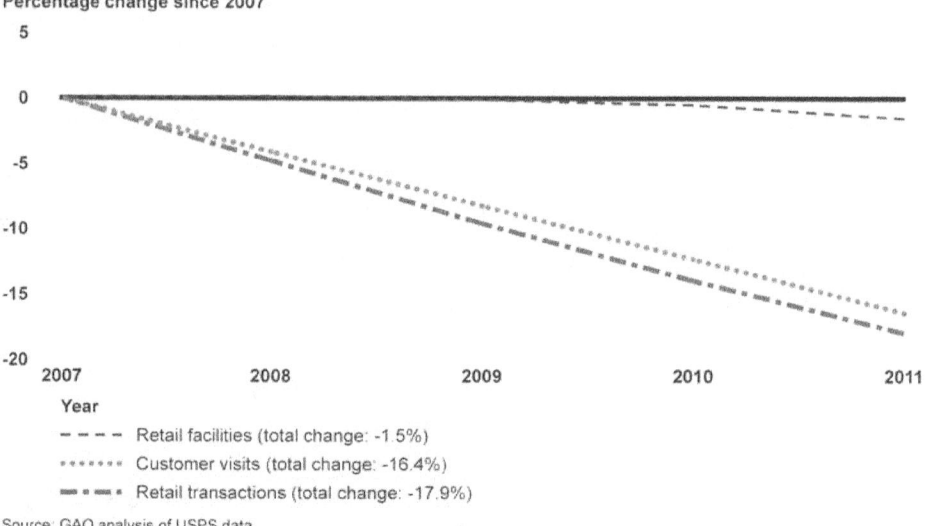

Percentage change since 2007

- - - - Retail facilities (total change: -1.5%)
.... Customer visits (total change: -16.4%)
— ▪ — ▪ Retail transactions (total change: -17.9%)

Source: GAO analysis of USPS data.

To address its financial crisis, the Postmaster General told Congress last September that USPS plans to reduce annual costs organization-wide by $20 billion—or 27 percent of its projected $73 billion total operating expenses—by fiscal year 2015.[5] One of the cost-savings initiatives he discussed was optimizing the retail network by reducing the number of USPS-operated facilities and increasing the number of lower-cost, alternative retail options, such as self-service kiosks and partnerships with retailers, that would preserve service close to where customers live,

---

[5]Statement of Postmaster General Patrick R. Donahoe before the Committee on Homeland Security and Governmental Affairs, United States Senate (Sept. 6, 2011).

GAO-12-433 U.S. Postal Service

work and shop. Currently, in addition to USPS-operated facilities, customers can purchase postal products or services at over 70,000 locations, including non-USPS-operated facilities consisting of 3,700 contract postal units and community post offices,[6] retailers that have partnered with USPS to sell postal products and services, and on its website.[7] Customers can also order supplies by phone and have packages picked up at their door.

The scale of the actions that USPS plans to take over the next 3 years is greater than anything it has previously undertaken. It plans to review approximately half of its retail facilities for possible closure, reduction in hours, and alternative access, including transfer of services to a contract unit or rural delivery service. In addition, USPS is exploring expansion of alterative access through such things as franchising opportunities and use of kiosks to create additional channels to access retail services. Some Members of Congress have raised concerns about these plans and the potential negative impact that closing post offices could have on affected communities. Congress has been considering several postal reform bills to put USPS on a path to financial viability, and some Members have asked USPS to postpone retail facility closures so as not to pre-empt congressional action on postal reform. In response, USPS agreed to place a moratorium on closing any postal retail facilities until May 15, 2012.

To help inform your consideration of actions needed to restructure USPS operations and help it achieve financial viability, you asked us to examine its retail network. This report discusses (1) key actions USPS has taken to restructure its retail network over the past 5 years; (2) concerns raised by postal stakeholders, including Congress, the Postal Regulatory Commission (PRC), USPS Office of Inspector General (OIG), and postal business and residential customers, and USPS's response to these concerns; and (3) the challenges that USPS faces in changing its retail network. To address these objectives, we reviewed USPS guidance and other documents on its retail actions and initiatives, as well as retail network goals, analyzed USPS retail network operating statistics from

---

[6]Contract postal units are operated by nonpostal employees in privately operated businesses, such as convenience stores, grocery stores, greeting card stores, and pharmacies. Community post offices are contract postal units that are located in small communities and function as main post offices.

[7]https://store.usps.com/store.

fiscal years 2007 to 2011, and interviewed agency officials responsible for managing and overseeing the retail network. Based on interviews with USPS staff about how they collect information and maintain their databases, we assessed the reliability of USPS data and noted limitations where appropriate. We also noted problems with data and analysis as reported by PRC and USPS OIG, and we analyzed regulatory proceedings, and proposed legislation addressing postal reform. We conducted site visits to the Arkansas and Colorado/Wyoming postal districts to observe public meetings[8] and obtain information on challenges to restructuring the retail network. We selected these sites based on several criteria, including the number and timing of upcoming public meetings and location.[9] We interviewed stakeholders relevant to retail network restructuring, including USPS officials involved in district reviews of proposed facility closures, PRC officials, and postmaster associations. We also reviewed laws, regulations, legislative proposals, and prior work by GAO, USPS OIG, PRC, and the Congressional Research Service.[10]

We conducted this performance audit from April 2011 to April 2012 in accordance with generally accepted government auditing standards. Those standards require that we plan and perform the audit to obtain sufficient, appropriate evidence to provide a reasonable basis for our findings and conclusions based on our audit objectives. We believe that the evidence obtained provides a reasonable basis for our findings and conclusions based on our audit objectives.

Background

USPS has a universal service obligation, part of which requires it to provide access to retail services. Several statutory provisions govern USPS when considering changes to its retail network, such as the following.

- Section 101 of Title 39 of the U.S. Code states, "The Postal Service shall have as its basic function the obligation to provide postal

---

[8]In addition to observing public meetings during site visits, we attended public meetings in Maryland, Virginia, and Washington, D.C.

[9]See appendix I for more information on our site visit selections.

[10]See appendix I for a more detailed description of our scope and methodology.

services to bind the Nation together through the personal, educational, literary, and business correspondence of the people."[11]

- USPS is required to serve the public and provide a maximum degree of effective and regular postal services to rural areas, communities, and small towns where post offices are not self-sustaining.[12]

- USPS is authorized to determine the need for post offices and to provide such offices as it determines are needed.[13]

- Regarding post offices, the law requires that no small post office shall be closed[14] solely for operating at a deficit,[15] and language in annual appropriations has provided that none of the appropriated funds shall be used to consolidate or close small rural and other small post offices.[16]

Further, before closing a post office or other USPS-operated retail facility, USPS must, among other steps, consider the effects on the communities served, its employees, and the services provided, as well as economic savings to be achieved, and it must provide customers with at least 60 days of notice before the proposed closure date. In addition, any person served by the post office may appeal its closure to PRC, and PRC has 120 days to affirm USPS's decision or remand it for further consideration.[17] However, the ultimate authority to close a post office rests with the USPS. A more-detailed discussion of USPS's process for

---

[11]39 U.S.C. § 101(a).

[12]39 U.S.C. § 101(b).

[13]39 U.S.C. § 404(a)(3).

[14]USPS guidance uses the term "discontinuance" to describe ending operations at a USPS-operated retail facility, such as a post office, station, or branch. Stations and branches are subordinate units of a main post office and generally offer the same products and services as post offices. Throughout this report, we use the term "closure," except when referring to USPS guidance.

[15]39 U.S.C. § 101(b).

[16]For example, see Pub. L. No. 112-74, 125 Stat. 786, 923 (Dec. 23, 2011).

[17]39 U.S.C. § 404(d)(5).

closing postal facilities is provided in a recent report by the Congressional Research Service.[18]

The size of USPS's retail network has remained largely unchanged over the past 5 years, although customer visits and transactions have declined, as shown in table 1.

Table 1: Retail Network Facts, Fiscal Years 2007-2011

Year	2007	2008	2009	2010	2011	Percentage change from 2007-2011
Total USPS-operated retail facilities	32,695	32,741	32,662	32,528	32,196	-1.5
Total non-USPS-operated retail facilities[a]	4,026	3,982	3,834	3,694	3,586	-10.9
Total retail transactions in USPS-operated retail facilities (in billions)[b]	2.51	2.39	2.27	2.16	2.06	-17.9
Total customer visits to USPS-operated retail facilities (in billions)[b]	1.22	1.17	1.12	1.07	1.02	-16.4

Source: USPS.

[a]Non-USPS operated includes contract postal units and community post offices.

[b]USPS does not track retail transactions and customer visits at all facilities. Therefore, USPS uses an extrapolation to determine the transaction and customer visit information for all USPS-operated retail locations.

In 2002, USPS released a transformation plan[19] that described challenges it faced with its retail network and optimization strategy. It also described plans to address these challenges—for example, by introducing retail alternatives in concert with reducing its retail network footprint and operating costs. USPS stated that it would "provide customers with easier and more convenient retail access. Postal services will be available where customers need them—at home, at work, where they shop, or at the post office. The Postal Service will promote the convenience of existing, underutilized alternatives and develop new low-cost solutions using technology, partnerships, and product simplification."

---

[18]Congressional Research Service, *The U.S. Postal Service: Common Questions about Post Office Closures*, R41950 (Washington, D.C: Jan. 13, 2012).

[19]*United States Postal Service Transformation Plan* (Washington, D.C.: April 2002).

In 2003, the President's Commission on the Postal Service issued a report that noted many of the nation's post offices were no longer necessary to fulfill USPS's universal service obligation, given the proliferation of alternative retail access points in grocery stores, drug stores, ATMs, and other more convenient locales in communities across the country.[20] The commission recommended that USPS maximize the potential of low-activity post offices by operating those necessary for fulfilling the universal service obligation, even if they operate at a substantial economic loss. However, where low-activity post offices are not necessary, it should have flexibility to dispose of them, with appropriate local community involvement, and existing statutes and appropriations that limit flexibility should be repealed.

We have said that network restructuring is a key action to help USPS reduce its costs and improve efficiency. In 2009, we suggested that USPS restructure its retail network to eliminate growing excess capacity, reduce costs, and improve efficiency.[21] Additionally, in 2011, we recommended that it develop a plan for optimizing its retail network that addresses both traditional post offices and retail alternatives.[22] A senior USPS official told us in January 2012 that USPS was in the process of developing a retail optimization plan.

In February 2012, USPS released a 5-year business plan, with an organization-wide goal to achieve $22.5 billion in annual cost savings through a combination of legislative and operational changes,[23] including $2 billion in savings from optimizing the retail network. According to USPS, it plans to reduce its total workforce of 557,000 employees by 155,000 within the next 5 years through attrition, as over half of its career employees are now retirement-eligible. The plan did not indicate how many of these proposed employee reductions would occur as a result of changes to its retail network.

---

[20]President's Commission on the United States Postal Service, *Embracing the Future: Making the Tough Choices to Preserve Universal Mail Service* (Washington, D.C.: July 31, 2003).

[21]GAO, *High Risk Series: Restructuring the U.S. Postal Service to Achieve Sustainable Financial Viability*, GAO-09-937SP (Washington, D.C. July 2009).

[22]GAO, *U.S. Postal Service: Action Needed to Maximize Cost-Saving Potential of Alternatives to Post Offices*, GAO-12-100 (Washington, D.C. Nov. 17, 2011).

[23]This 5-year business plan is separate from the USPS's retail optimization plan.

USPS Has Taken Several Actions to Restructure Its Retail Network

Over the past 5 years, USPS has taken several actions to change its retail network through reducing its workforce and retail footprints, while expanding retail alternatives. It estimated that it saved about $800 million by reducing retail work hours during this period.[24] It also closed 631 of its post offices, but it did not have cost savings estimates related to these closures. Further, most of the facilities closed (500) were post offices where operations had first been suspended due to emergencies or a postmaster vacancy. Fewer closures (131) have resulted from the nationwide reviews that USPS initiated in 2009 and 2011.

Retail Workforce Reductions

Over the past 5 years, USPS reduced the number of retail clerks by 26 percent and the number of postmasters by 7.4 percent at USPS-operated facilities, as shown in table 2. It also created a new noncareer postal support employee position, whose wages will be approximately one-third of a clerk's average wage.[25] An agreement reached with the American Postal Workers Union in May 2011 allows USPS to increase its use of noncareer employees by up to 20 percent of clerk positions covered by the agreement. In related efforts to cut costs, USPS has reduced total retail work hours of clerks and postmasters by about 20 percent since fiscal year 2006 through employee attrition and schedule adaptation.

Table 2: USPS-Operated Retail Network Workforce, Fiscal Years 2007-2011

Year	2007	2008	2009	2010	2011	Percentage change from 2007-2011
Number of postmasters	25,285	25,250	23,672	23,111	23,426	-7.4
Number of retail clerks	41,086	39, 297	35,321	32,089	30,393	-26.0
Number of retail work hours (in millions)[a]	106.4	103.2	94.1	87.7	85.1	-20.0

Source: USPS.

[a]This number includes postmaster and clerk hours dedicated to retail operations.

[24]In responding to questions about retail savings, USPS provided cost-savings data related to retail work-hour reductions only. We requested annual cost-savings data related to specific facilities and initiatives for fiscal years 2007 through 2011, but USPS did not provide this information.

[25]USPS reports that an average hourly rate for a clerk is $42.40, whereas a postal support employee will be paid $14.60 per hour.

Retail Footprint Reduction

During the past 5 years, USPS designed two nationwide initiatives—known as the Station and Branch Optimization Initiative (2009 Retail Initiative) and the Retail Access Optimization Initiative (2011 Retail Initiative)—to review (1) over 3,000 USPS-operated retail facilities in urban and suburban areas and (2) about 3,650 primarily rural facilities for possible closure. Table 3 describes key information about these initiatives.

Table 3: Summary of USPS Retail Closure Initiatives and Actions

Initiative	Time frame	Objective	Action	Results
Station and Branch Optimization and Consolidation Initiative	Began in 2009. Completed in 2011.	Identify and take advantage of opportunities for increased efficiency while also ensuring that USPS maintains postal facilities of such character and in such locations that postal patrons have ready access to postal services.	Over 3,000 large stations and branches, primarily in urban and suburban areas, were to be considered for potential closure. This population was reduced by district-led prescreening to approximately 760 facilities.	Closed 131 stations and branches by the end of fiscal year 2011.
Retail Access Optimization Initiative	Began in 2011. Initiative is ongoing, but closures are on hold.	Evaluate the postal retail network to determine whether the number of facilities could be reduced while maintaining postal facilities needed to provide postal customers with ready access to postal services consistent with reasonable economies of postal operations.	Headquarters officials produced a list of facilities to be studied for potential closure using data-driven criteria; districts then conducted closure studies. A majority of the approximately 3,650 facilities to be studied were low-revenue, low-workload small post offices in rural areas.	Due to the December 2011 moratorium on USPS retail facility closures, no facilities have yet been closed under this initiative. The moratorium is scheduled to be lifted on May 15, 2012.

Source: GAO analysis of USPS data.

In addition, over the last 5 years, USPS district offices have identified and closed around 500 USPS-operated retail facilities on an individual, ad-hoc basis as they determined the need.[26] These individual closures were in response to a postmaster vacancy or the suspension of operations due to

---

[26]USPS has 7 area and 67 district offices throughout the United States. Officials at the district offices are charged with conducting studies on closing USPS-operated retail facilities.

an expired lease or irreparable damage to the facility following a natural disaster. Many of these closures were for facilities that had suspended operations years ago, but USPS did not formally close the facility until recently.

Alternative Retail Expansion

USPS has continued to expand the number and type of alternatives at which customers can access retail postal products and services outside of USPS-operated postal facilities. These alternatives include self-service options as well as partnerships with retailers, which could help it contain facility and labor costs while still providing access for customers. Examples of retail alternatives include its website, self-service kiosks, contract postal units, rural carrier services, approved shippers, Village Post Offices,[27] stamp retailers, orders of supplies by telephone, and package pickup at the door. The percentage of retail revenue from these alternatives increased from 24 percent in 2007 to 35 percent in 2011, as shown in table 4. USPS has projected that by 2020, alternatives to USPS-operated retail facilities may account for 60 percent of its retail revenue.

Table 4: USPS Retail Alternative Revenue Changes, Fiscal Years 2007-2011

Year	2007	2008	2009	2010	2011	Percentage change from 2007-2011
Total retail revenue (in billions)	$18.5	$18.7	$17.7	$17.5	$17.0	-8.1
Retail revenue from alternatives (in billions)	$4.4	$4.5	$5.0	$5.4	$6.0	+ 36.4
Percentage revenue from alternative retail	24	24	28	31	35	+46.0

Source: USPS.

---

[27]The Village Post Office was announced by USPS at the same time it began the 2011 Retail Initiative. Village Post Offices will be non-USPS operated facilities that offer a range of postal products and services that could include stamps, post office boxes, prepaid flat rate shipping boxes, and envelopes. They are meant for communities that either have no existing post office or that could be affected by ongoing postal facility closure studies.

Stakeholders Have Expressed Concerns about USPS Retail Initiatives

Postal stakeholders, including Members of Congress, PRC, USPS OIG, customers, employee associations, and some community residents have raised concerns about USPS's retail restructuring initiatives. These concerns include

- access to postal services, including community residents' ability to obtain retail services, the adequacy of retail alternatives, and changes to delivery services;

- the impact of facility closures on communities;

- the adequacy of data analysis of facilities facing closure and the reliability of data, particularly with regard to the accuracy of cost-savings estimates;

- the transparency and equity of closure decisions;

- the fairness of facility closure procedures; and

- changes in who can manage a post office.

Access to Postal Services

USPS regulations provide that local management host a community meeting to obtain public input when it proposes to close a facility.[28] One of the major concerns of community residents at meetings we attended was that the communities' access to postal services would decline if USPS closed the facility and the next closest postal facility was too far. For example, at a meeting we attended in Colorado, one resident described the community as "isolated" and expressed concern that the distance to the next closest post office (about 25 miles) was unreasonable. Another resident stated that should the post office close, driving about 50 miles round-trip to mail packages was not a viable option. At another site we visited in Arkansas, postal officials told us that proximity of all post offices is one of the major factors they consider when reviewing facilities on the 2011 Retail Initiative study list.

At meetings we attended, community residents also raised questions about the adequacy of other available alternatives. For example, one

---

[28]39 C.F.R. § 241.3(d)(3).

Page 11   GAO-12-433 U.S. Postal Service resident said that he could not access retail services on USPS's website because Internet service was not available. Additional concerns about retail alternatives were raised by PRC. In the 2011 Retail Initiative, PRC questioned whether USPS had adequate alternative retail access options available for retail facilities that it proposed closing. PRC said that alternative access should be considered concurrently with closure studies and be presently available. Postal officials at the meetings we attended encouraged customers to provide feedback on proposed retail alternatives, and USPS officials told us they have attempted to coordinate expanding alternatives with closures. They gave the example of introducing the concept of partnering with local businesses to create a Village Post Office[29] along with the announcement of the 2011 Retail Initiative. However, Village Post Offices may not offer a realistic alternative for customers in some rural areas because there may not be businesses in the community to host a post office. As of January 2012, nine Village Post Offices were in operation, and 13 others were under contract, according to USPS.

Citizens in the rural communities we visited also had concerns about how mail delivery, including post office box locations and addresses would change if USPS closed the community's postal facility. USPS officials presented rural route service as an alternative, acknowledging that it could require an address change. In addition, according to officials, because some customers may not meet the requirements to receive rural route delivery, they may have to go to another post office to pick up their mail. Some community members who used post office boxes as their only mode of delivery were worried about the inconvenience of having to travel further to another postal facility to pick up their mail.[30] Several customers

---

[29]With Village Post Offices, USPS intends to partner with existing businesses, town halls, or government centers to provide a limited array of postal products and services to the local community, including mail collection boxes, post office boxes, stamps, and flat-rate shipping and mailing products. USPS launched its first Village Post Office in the town of Malone, Washington, in the summer of 2011.

[30]Per USPS policy, postal residential customers receive one free form of mail delivery in the United States. In places where USPS does not provide carrier delivery, free post office box delivery is provided. Some remote areas do not have rural delivery routes and therefore receive free post office box delivery.

stated that if their post office were to close, they would prefer having some postal physical presence in their town, such as cluster boxes.[31]

Impact on Communities

We observed USPS and its customers sometimes had varied expectations about its role in the community. For example, community residents in one small town stated that they were concerned about loss of community identity if the post office were to close.

Appeals filed with the PRC highlight issues similar to those brought up at community meetings. For example, various appeals that we examined included concerns that

- losing the local post office would have a negative impact on community, including loss of identity and inhibiting economic growth;

- because USPS did not have accurate information about the community, customers believed USPS did not have complete information about the community's needs.

- USPS had not allowed for adequate community input; at public meetings, residents perceived that a decision had already been made about the closure; and

- residents believed that the available alternatives were not adequate or were too inconvenient.

In written responses to customer concerns in appeals cases, USPS has indicated that community identity comes from the interest and vitality of its residents and that it would still help to preserve the identity by maintaining a community's ZIP Code. At one community meeting we attended, a postal official told those in attendance that the community's identity is not dependent on the post office. USPS has responded to concerns about the economic effects of closures by stating that businesses require regular and effective service, which would be provided to them by the alternative offered to replace the closing facility. It also indicated that its analysis of customer questionnaires helps to determine if the potential change would

---

[31]Cluster box units are a centralized grouping of individually locked and keyed compartments or mailboxes, such as a wall-mounted unit in an apartment building or a freestanding neighborhood delivery and collection box unit.

have a negative impact on local businesses by asking whether customers would continue to use those businesses in the event of a facility closure. Postal officials we spoke with noted that they used the responses to customer questionnaires to see where customers obtained other services, such as buying groceries, to figure out which alternative locations could offer community residents convenient access to postal services.

Adequacy of USPS Analysis and Data

Another issue the PRC and other stakeholders raised was related to the adequacy of USPS's analysis and data. For example, in the 2009 Retail Initiative, the PRC recommended that USPS improve its financial analysis to better reflect potential revenue declines and operational expenses that may result from closing a post office. In the 2011 Retail Initiative proceeding, USPS reported that it had improved its financial analysis model, generating data that it determined would provide a better assessment of cost savings than the previous model. Despite the change, PRC's 2011 Retail Initiative advisory opinion[32] stated that it was unable to develop a reasonable estimate of the financial impact of the initiative because USPS did not collect facility-specific revenue and cost data or separate retail costs from other operational costs.

In addition to questions about the overall financial impact of initiatives, the adequacy of USPS's cost-savings estimates for individual facilities has also been questioned by the PRC during the appeals process.[33] In fiscal year 2011, in six of the nine cases that PRC remanded—that is, where the PRC sent the cases back to USPS for further consideration—PRC either found that USPS did not adequately consider economic savings and asked USPS to clarify aspects of its estimate upon remand or cited related concerns such as overestimating savings from postmaster salaries or leases.

---

[32]Whenever USPS proposes a change in the nature of postal services that affects service on a nationwide basis, USPS must request an advisory opinion on the change from PRC. 39 U.S.C. § 3661(b).

[33]When USPS makes a decision to close or consolidate a post office, customers of the post office may appeal the decision to PRC. 39 U.S.C. § 404(d)(5). PRC may affirm the decision or remand it to USPS for further consideration. USPS and PRC do not agree on whether PRC has jurisdiction over appeals for station and branches.

PRC, USPS OIG, and we have raised concerns about USPS's retail network data.[34] PRC outlined concerns and recommendations, including in the following examples, about USPS's data pertaining to its retail network in its advisory opinion on the 2011 Retail Initiative.

- USPS does not collect cost and revenue data separately for post offices, stations, and branches. Additionally, operating costs for retail activities cannot be separated from nonretail operating costs, restricting USPS's ability to estimate the potential cost savings from closures because it makes it difficult to determine the actual costs associated with individual retail facilities.

- USPS does not collect the data to measure revenue lost due to closures, restricting the ability to perform a post-implementation analysis on the net financial impact of closures. Postal officials told us they were in the process of creating a tool that would estimate total demand for retail postal services by geographic area and account for the revenue and cost implications of alternatives.

- PRC found that USPS should develop a method to measure how successfully it met its goals for the 2011 Retail Initiative and that it should attempt to coordinate and estimate the impact of all relevant initiatives that could affect customer access to services. This analysis would also help ensure that the right data are collected to measure stated goals. USPS officials told us that although they have looked at the overall effect on customers, they are unable to predict which initiatives will eventually be implemented, as some require statutory change and therefore they have examined the impact of each initiative independently.

Additional data concerns that we and the USPS OIG have raised include the following:

- In November 2011, we reported that USPS lacks performance measures and data needed to know the extent to which customers are aware of and willing to use its various retail alternatives.[35] We also

---

[34]See, for example, GAO-12-100; and GAO, *U.S. Postal Service Facilities: Improvements in Data Would Strengthen Maintenance and Alignment of Access to Retail Services*, GAO-08-41 (Washington, D.C. Dec. 10, 2007).

[35]GAO-12-100.

spoke with USPS officials about customer data, and they stated that transaction data and customer visits are not tracked in electronic databases for some small post offices—approximately 10 percent of the total retail facilities it operates. Lack of tracking makes it difficult to match alternatives to the services that customers are demanding or using at small post offices. A USPS official commented that it is developing a strategic retail plan that includes a charter designed to provide greater convenience, lower-cost service, and improve the customer experience, but it is unclear how this plan will address the lack of data at small post offices.

- In December 2011, the USPS OIG recommended that USPS improve the reliability and usefulness of retail facilities data by validating, correcting, and updating information in its retail facility database.[36] Moreover, we have also recommended improvements to USPS's retail facilities data.[37] In both cases, USPS agreed to implement the recommendations related to the facilities data.

Transparency and Equity Concerns Raised about USPS Closure Decisions

Recent USPS OIG analyses of the 2009 and 2011 Retail Initiatives found that USPS could make improvements in establishing clear criteria for evaluating closure decisions and implementing an integrated retail network strategy that includes short- and long-term plans, milestones, and goals. USPS OIG found that these improvements could raise stakeholders' confidence that USPS will make transparent, equitable, and fact-based decisions.[38] USPS agreed with the findings in these reports but noted that a "one-size-fits-all" approach might not take factors about the local community into account and that its retail operations will never be uniform across the entire network.

Other customers raised equity issues with USPS's decisions. For example, some people in a small community at a public meeting we attended viewed rural post offices as bearing the brunt of closures and viewed urban areas as not being equally affected. Customers also

---

[36]U.S. Postal Service Office of Inspector General, *Postal Service-Operated Retail Facilities Discontinuance Program*, EN-AR-12-002 (Washington, D.C.: Dec. 2011).

[37]GAO-08-41.

[38]For example, see U.S. Postal Service Office of Inspector General, *Stations and Branches Optimization and Consolidation Initiative*, EN-AR-10-005 (Aug. 17, 2010).

wanted clarification on the criteria used to decide which facilities would be studied and whether other closure initiatives would affect their service. Similarly, in an appeals case, customers expressed concerns that the nearest post office was also being studied for closure and that if both facilities were closed, they would have to travel even further to obtain services.

Fairness in Facility Closure Procedures

PRC raised a concern in its 2009 Retail Initiative advisory opinion that USPS was not providing customers of stations and branches with the same rights as customers of post offices in a closure proceeding. The advisory opinion also noted that the public does not really understand the distinction between various facility types and it is confusing to have procedures for stations and branches that are different for post offices. Further, PRC found that stations and branches fulfill the same operational purposes as post offices and recommended that USPS provide similar treatment to customers if their local station, branch, or post office were closed. In another PRC proceeding in 2010, PRC raised a similar concern about the practice of suspending operations at offices for extended periods without giving the public the right to comment as would be afforded in a formal closure study.[39] At some facilities, USPS suspended services and took no further action to restore service or proceed with closure for, at times, many years.

In response to PRC concerns, USPS made several changes, including as part of the 2011 Retail Initiative and in district office-initiated post office closures that began after July 2011. These changes included the following:

- *Implementing uniform closure procedures for all USPS-operated retail facilities.* USPS developed standards that were finalized in July 2011 to address internal and public confusion over different discontinuance procedures.[40]

- *Clarifying circumstances that can prompt a closure study.* New regulations allow USPS headquarters to identify USPS-operated retail facilities for studies and also provide details on the particular

---

[39]Investigation of Suspended Post Offices, Docket No. PI2010-1.

[40]76 *Fed. Reg.* 41413 (July 14, 2011).

circumstances that can prompt a study.[41] These circumstances include: a postmaster vacancy, an emergency suspension, low-workload levels, insufficient customer demand, and the availability of reasonable alternative access to postal services.[42]

- *Creating a web-based data program to guide closure studies.* USPS created this program and incorporated it into its closure processes as of December 2010. The program is used to collect information, such as all community comments during the closure process, and to guide USPS along a series of required steps. According to USPS, the web-based program has helped streamline the overall closure process and improved the internal tracking of facility closures, including customer comments and community statistics, such as the number of businesses in the community and the nearest retail alternatives.

- *Clarifying procedures for reviewing facilities where operations have undergone emergency suspensions.* USPS issued revised guidance in July 2011,[43] affirming that customers of facilities that have undergone emergency suspensions must be allowed an opportunity to comment on the proposed discontinuance.[44] This provision addressed long-standing concerns of stakeholders regarding postal facilities where USPS suspends services for long periods of time.

In addition, there has been a sharp increase recently in the number of appeals filed with PRC related to USPS decisions to close or consolidate a post office. In fiscal year 2010, 6 appeals were filed with PRC. In fiscal year 2011, PRC received more than 100 post office closing appeals and 100 were filed in the first quarter of fiscal year 2012. To expedite the appeals process, PRC streamlined and simplified its procedures for reviewing appeals and simplified the process to make it easier for the

---

[41]39 C.F.R. § 241.3(a)(5).

[42]In the 2009 Retail Initiative, USPS headquarters supplied USPS district officials with a population of facilities and charged the district officials to determine which facilities to study for closure.

[43]*Postal Service-Operated Retail Facilities Discontinuance Guide* (Handbook PO-101).

[44]An emergency suspension of a post office's operations occurs due to circumstances such as a natural disaster, loss of the post office building lease when no suitable alternative location is available, or severe damage to or destruction of the post office building.

public to participate in and to understand PRC's decision-making process.[45]

Changes in Who Can Manage Post Offices

USPS also changed its regulations related to the staffing of post offices. Previously, a postmaster was the only employee who could manage operations at a post office. New regulations now allow post offices to be operated or staffed by other types of postal employees,[46] who would be paid less than postmasters and would report to a postmaster. USPS expects that this change would give it more staffing flexibility, reduce the number of postmasters, and reduce costs. A USPS official explained that changes in operations, such as the removal of delivery operations from some retail facilities, have resulted in a decreased level of responsibility for some postmasters over time. Postmasters filed a complaint with PRC about these proposed changes.[47] The PRC dismissed this complaint because it was filed before this provision of the proposed rule was finalized.

Challenges Restrict USPS from Changing Its Retail Network

USPS faces challenges such as legal restrictions and resistance from some Members of Congress and the public that have limited its ability to restructure its network. Also, certain policy issues are unresolved, and pending legislation takes differing approaches to resolving USPS's challenges.

Legal Restrictions and Resistance

Some legal restrictions have presented challenges to USPS's plans to restructure its retail network. As described in the background section of this report, the law states that no small post office shall be closed solely for operating at a deficit.[48] Further, language in annual appropriations acts has provided that none of the funds appropriated in the acts (about $100 million for fiscal year 2011) shall be used to consolidate or close small

---

[45]See 77 *Fed. Reg.* 6676 (Feb. 9, 2012).

[46]39 C.F.R. § 241.1(a).

[47]Specifically, commenters expressed the view that the Postmasters Equity Act precluded the proposed change that a post office may be staffed by nonpostmaster personnel. 76 *Fed. Reg.* 41413 (July 14, 2011).

[48]39 U.S.C. § 101(b).

rural and other small post offices.[49] On one hand, USPS is supposed to "act like a business" and be self-financing, but on the other hand, it is restricted by law from making decisions that businesses would commonly make, such as closing unprofitable units.

In addition to these statutory restrictions, USPS faces resistance from some Members of Congress and the public who oppose some facility closures. For example, at some public meetings we attended, staff from some congressional offices spoke to community members about actions they could take to challenge potential closures. For example, they encouraged residents to write letters to their Members of Congress and cite specific, negative impacts a potential closing might have. At one community meeting, congressional staffers said they had received several letters from community members. In response to such actions by constituents, many Members of Congress have written letters to USPS requesting that it not close post offices in their districts. In December 2011, 20 Senators signed a letter to Senate leaders requesting that they consider including language in an appropriations bill that would prevent USPS from closing any rural post offices until Congress has passed reform legislation. USPS then placed a moratorium on all facility closures until May 15, 2012, while Congress considers postal reform bills. USPS has encouraged Congress to enact postal reform legislation that would provide USPS with more flexibility to make retail closure decisions by eliminating statutory restrictions. Further, USPS officials told us that in response to resistance to closures, they are considering reducing post office operating hours rather than closing some facilities.

Certain Policy Issues and Pending Legislation

Pending postal reform legislation provides an opportunity for Congress to address certain unresolved policy issues related to USPS's retail restructuring plans. These policy issues include

- what level or type of retail services should USPS provide to meet customers' changing use of postal services;

- how should the cost of these services be paid;

---

[49]For example, see Pub. L. No. 112-74, 125 Stat. 786, 923 (Dec. 23, 2011). Generally, USPS has received annual appropriations for revenue forgone by providing free mail for the blind and for overseas voters.

GAO-12-433 U.S. Postal Service

- how should USPS restructure its operations, networks, and workforce to support changes in services; and

- how should Congress provide USPS with flexibility to restructure its networks and workforce while still holding USPS accountable to Congress and the public?

Several bills related to postal reform have been introduced in the 112th Congress, and two have been approved by the Senate and House oversight committees—S. 1789 and H.R. 2309.[50] As seen in the following two examples, these bills provide different approaches to addressing the legal restrictions and resistance USPS faces to closing facilities and the unresolved policy issues.

- S. 1789 requires USPS to establish retail service standards and consider several factors before making a closure decision, including consolidating with another facility, reducing hours of operation, and procuring a contract to provide retail services within the community. The bill also allows USPS to provide retail alternatives to dedicated post offices but also puts in place considerations before closing post offices.

- H.R. 2309 removes the statutory restriction on post office closures "solely for operating at a deficit" and establishes a commission similar to the Base Realignment and Closure Commission.[51] USPS would submit a plan to the commission, which would then make closure recommendations to Congress that would be implemented unless Congress passed a joint resolution of disapproval.

Table 5 summarizes several challenges to restructuring the retail network and some options to address these challenges that are included in these bills.

---

[50]21st Century Postal Service Act of 2011 S. 1789, 112th Cong. (2011) and Postal Reform Act of 2011, H.R. 2309, 112th Cong. (2011).

[51]The Base Realignment and Closure Commission was established to realign military installations within the United States.

Table 5: Summary of Challenges to Restructuring USPS Retail Network and Proposed Options

Category	Challenges	Options
Statutory requirements related to universal service	• Restrictions on closing post offices solely for operating at a deficit and provisions for providing a "maximum degree of regular and effective service" in rural areas must be balanced against requirements for USPS to achieve efficiencies and be self-financing. • Language in annual appropriations has provided that none of the appropriated funds shall be used to consolidate or close small rural and other small post offices. • No specific retail service standards exist in law, resulting in varied expectations of how USPS should meet its universal service obligations as it makes changes to its retail network.	• H.R. 2309[a] strikes the "maximum degree" language and restrictions on small post offices closures "solely for operating at a deficit." • H.R. 2309 requires USPS to provide effective and regular postal services to rural areas, communities, and small towns where post offices are not self-sustaining. It provides that a post office closure cannot be appealed if a contract postal unit is opened within two miles of the post office. • S. 1789[b] requires USPS's network plan to ensure that small communities and rural areas continue to receive "regular and effective access to retail postal services." Further it requires USPS, where possible, to provide for improved customer access to postal services. • S. 1789 requires USPS to define service standards while taking into consideration certain factors such as the proximity of retail services to customers and the transportation challenges in the area served.
Congressional and other stakeholder resistance to USPS facility closures	• Members of Congress have raised concerns about USPS decisions that could affect facilities in the areas they represent, as well as with USPS's overall network plan. Additionally, some Members have opposed USPS's plans to close retail facilities in their districts. A group of Senators requested a moratorium to delay further closures until the Senate can consider USPS's plans and pending legislation. USPS responded by placing a moratorium on closures until May 15, 2012.	• S. 1789 prohibits closures, except for health or safety issues, until retail standards are established. It requires USPS to consider several options before making a closure decision, including consolidating with another facility, reducing hours of operation, and procuring a contract to provide retail services within the community. • S. 1789 allows USPS to provide retail alternatives to dedicated post offices, but also puts in place considerations before closing post offices. • H.R. 2309 establishes a commission similar to the Base Realignment and Closure Commission. USPS submits a plan to an independent third party (the Commission on Postal Reorganization) that makes closure recommendations to Congress that are implemented unless a joint resolution of disapproval is passed. • H.R. 2309 requires USPS, in consultation with PRC, to submit a plan for retail closures and consolidations that would result in total savings of at least $1 billion.

Source: GAO analysis of pending legislation.

[a]Postal Reform Act of 2011, H.R. 2309, 112th Cong. (2011).

[b]21st Century Postal Service Act of 2011 S. 1789, 112th Cong. (2011).

Concluding Observations

USPS must carefully work to ensure a viable strategy to effectively size its retail network to reduce costs to match declining mail volume while maintaining access to retail services. It is clear that USPS cannot support its current level of services and operations from its current revenues. USPS's ability to continue providing its current level of services is in jeopardy, and it is up to both Congress and USPS to construct solutions that will either reduce the cost of services or increase revenues from other sources. But it appears that USPS cannot restructure its retail network unless Congress addresses USPS's financial instability and the long-standing challenges that hinder its ability to change its retail network. If Congress prefers to retain the current level of service and associated network, decisions will need to be made about how USPS's costs for providing these services will be paid, including additional cost reductions or revenue sources. Because USPS is in the process of responding to several retail restructuring recommendations that its OIG, the PRC, and we have made, we are not making any additional recommendations.

Agency Comments

USPS provided written comments on a draft of this report by a letter dated April 11, 2012. USPS agreed with our findings, noting limitations management faces to restructuring. Further, it observed that its operating model is unsustainable and that maintaining the same level of retail services will require solutions to cover the costs of those services either through cost reductions or revenue enhancements. USPS also provided us with technical comments that were incorporated into the final version of this report as appropriate. USPS's comments are reprinted in appendix II.

We are sending copies of this report to the appropriate congressional committees, the Postmaster General, and other interested parties. In addition, the report is available at no charge on GAO's website at http://www.gao.gov.

If you or your staffs have any questions about this report, please contact me at (202) 512-2834 or stjamesl@gao.gov. Contact points for our Offices of Congressional Relations and Public Affairs may be found on the last page of this report. Key contributors to the report are listed in appendix III.

Lorelei St. James
Director
Physical Infrastructure Issues

Appendix I: Objectives, Scope, and Methodology

To help inform your consideration of actions needed to restructure U.S. Postal Service (USPS) operations and help it achieve financial viability, you asked us to examine USPS's retail network. This report discusses (1) key actions USPS has taken to restructure its retail network over the past 5 years; (2) concerns raised by postal stakeholders, including Congress, the Postal Regulatory Commission (PRC), USPS Office of Inspector General (OIG), and postal business and residential customers, and USPS's response to these concerns; and (3) the challenges that USPS faces in changing its retail network.

To determine what key actions USPS has taken to restructure its retail network, we reviewed documents related to the Station and Branch Optimization and Consolidation (2009 Retail Initiative) and Retail Access Optimization (2011 Retail Initiative), retail alternatives, and individual district-initiated discontinuances. We examined criteria and goals of the initiatives, the number of facilities studied, and the number of facilities closed. In describing trends in the number of USPS-operated facilities, retail transactions, and other retail operating statistics, we

- reviewed reports from USPS OIG and documents filed in several dockets from PRC related to the 2009 and 2011 Retail Initiatives, and other discontinuance procedures in general. We also reviewed past GAO work on the development of retail alternatives.

- reviewed USPS documents, including guidance for discontinuance processes, background documents on major initiatives, and overall goals for the retail network. Our review included examining rule changes between old and new discontinuance procedures.

- interviewed USPS officials who oversee retail network restructuring to discuss background of initiatives, criteria used for closures, discontinuance processes, and relevant data.

- reviewed USPS data from fiscal years 2006-2011 on the facilities, costs of the retail network, employees, and customer statistics to show trends in number of retail facilities, retail revenues, and operating costs over the past 5 years. We also requested estimates and projections for fiscal year 2015.

To understand the context of data provided by USPS, we spoke with knowledgeable officials to get a more-detailed understanding of how databases are used by officials and USPS's methodology for collecting information. We observed a demonstration of USPS's Change Suspension

Discontinuance Center program, which contains all of the information used during the discontinuance process. This demonstration gave us an idea of how district officials would use the program in support of discontinuance activities. We also interviewed USPS officials to discuss data we requested, including how variables were collected, and the methodology for cost-savings estimates and future projections. For customer visits and retail transaction data, we used an extrapolation provided by USPS since it does not collect data for some small post offices. We also reviewed variables used to estimate cost savings for individual facilities and the overall cost savings USPS provided us for the retail facility closures from fiscal years 2007 through 2011. We assessed the reliability of USPS data and noted, where appropriate, the limitations of certain data. For example, we requested annual cost-savings data related to USPS retail facility closures for fiscal years 2007 through 2011. USPS initially provided us with aggregate annual cost savings, but because it did not provide disaggregated data, we were not able to assess the reliability of these data. We also discuss in this report the problems with USPS data and analysis as reported by PRC and the USPS OIG.

To identify concerns raised by postal stakeholders and to determine what challenges USPS faces in restructuring its retail network, we analyzed past work by GAO, USPS OIG, and PRC as well as statutory requirements regarding facility closures and access to retail services. We also identified stakeholder concerns, both from communities and Members of Congress, that contributed to resistance to closures and reviewed proposed legislation to identify potential options for addressing retail network restructuring. We also discussed challenges to retail network restructuring with USPS and PRC officials. For example, when PRC attempted to estimate the costs and savings of the 2011 Retail Initiative, it reported it was unable to develop a reasonable estimate of the financial impact of the 2011 Retail Initiative because USPS did not collect facility-specific revenue and cost data or separate retail costs from other operational costs. In addition to questions about the overall financial impact of initiatives, the adequacy of USPS's cost-savings estimates for individual facilities has also been questioned by PRC during the appeals process.

- To obtain information on stakeholder issues raised by customers during past facility closures and USPS's communication, we conducted an analysis of the PRC appeals docket for fiscal year 2011. We examined reasons why facility closures were appealed, alternatives given by USPS to replace services provided at closed facilities, customer

concerns and USPS's responses to the concerns contained in the
administrative record, and PRC's analyses of the cases.

- To obtain information on stakeholder concerns for the ongoing 2011
  Retail Initiative and recommendations for improving the initiative, we
  conducted an analysis of the Nature of Service docket on the 2011
  Retail Initiative and the resulting PRC advisory opinion. We examined
  USPS testimony, briefs, and responses to interrogatories,
  summarized major issues brought up by stakeholders (including
  unions, postmaster groups, the National Newspaper Association, and
  the Public Representative), and examined the PRC advisory opinion
  to inform GAO findings on challenges to making progress in
  optimizing the retail network.

- To obtain information on resistance to closing facilities, we observed
  congressional hearings and community meetings, reviewed relevant
  news articles about congressional resistance to closures, and
  interviewed USPS and PRC officials.

To observe stakeholder concerns firsthand, we conducted site visits to
USPS districts to attend public meetings and to obtain detailed
information on discontinuance procedures, including criteria for closures
and the 2009 and 2011 Retail Initiatives. We chose two sites to visit, the
Arkansas and Colorado/Wyoming districts, based on the following criteria:

- number of upcoming public meetings,

- 2011 Retail Initiative study category,

- time range of meetings,

- proximity of meetings to district offices or cities, and

- cost and convenience of travel.

After applying these criteria to choose site visit locations, we attended two
to three community meetings per location and met with various district
officials to discuss the district-level discontinuance review process and
challenges to closing retail facilities. District officials we met with included:
district discontinuance coordinators, managers of marketing, managers of
customer and industry, and managers of post office operations. When
possible, we met with other relevant stakeholders during the site visits to
further our understanding of issues to facility closures. In Arkansas, we

spoke with a small business owner who had filed a petition for appeal of a closure in a suburban area. In Colorado, we spoke with senior postal officials in USPS's Western area office.

In addition to conducting site visits to areas that had predominantly small post offices, we also attended community meetings in urban areas for stations and branches. In total, we attended 10 community meetings at the following locations:

- Ivan, AR, Post Office.

- Jacksonport, AR, Post Office.

- Conejos, CO, Post Office.

- Chama, CO, Post Office.

- Jaroso, CO, Post Office.

- Theological Seminary Station in Alexandria, VA.

- Leisure World Station in Aspen Hill, MD.

- Market Center Station in Baltimore, MD.

- T Street and Kalorama Stations in Washington, D.C. (2 meetings).

Five meetings were for small post offices we observed during site visits, and 5 were for suburban or urban stations and branches in the Washington, D.C., area. To analyze which concerns were raised most frequently at the meetings we attended, we recorded all of the questions and comments made by customers during all of the meetings we attended.

To examine options for addressing challenges to restructuring the retail network, we compared provisions in several pieces of proposed postal reform legislation. We also spoke with USPS officials to discuss how to get an update on their ongoing initiatives, current options to achieve cost savings in the retail network, and their strategy for the retail network, including the integration of retail alternatives with facility closure initiatives.

We conducted this performance audit from April 2011 to April 2012 in accordance with generally accepted government auditing standards. Those standards require that we plan and perform the audit to obtain

sufficient, appropriate evidence to provide a reasonable basis for our
findings and conclusions based on our audit objectives. We believe that
the evidence obtained provides a reasonable basis for our findings and
conclusions based on our audit objectives.

Appendix II: Comments from the U.S. Postal Service

DEAN J. GRANHOLM
VICE PRESIDENT
DELIVERY AND POST OFFICE OPERATIONS

UNITED STATES POSTAL SERVICE

April 11, 2012

Ms. Lorelei St. James
Director, Physical Infrastructure Issues
United States Government Accountability Office
Washington, DC 20548-0001

Dear Ms. St. James,

The U.S. Postal Service (USPS) is pleased to offer comments on the Government Accountability Office (GAO) Report on *Actions, Issues, and Challenges to Restructuring the Postal Service's Retail Network*. The report identifies numerous challenges that the USPS confronts in its effort to implement initiatives to provide retail and delivery services conveniently and efficiently to the American public.

We agree with the GAO finding that postal management's ability to restructure the retail network is severely hampered by the USPS financial instability and other factors that limit flexibility in decision making. Further, we agree that in order to provide the same level of service to communities, solutions must be developed to cover the cost of that level of service, either through cost reductions or revenue enhancements. To do otherwise would perpetuate the Postal Service's unsustainable operating model, and prevent the USPS from executing its responsibility to provide prompt, reliable, and efficient service to patrons throughout the country.

If I can be of further assistance, or provide you with any further information, please do not hesitate to contact me at (202) 268-4359.

Thank for your consideration of these comments.

Sincerely,

Dean J. Granholm

475 L'ENFANT PLAZA SW
ROOM 7017
WASHINGTON, DC 20260-7017
202-268-8500
FAX: 202-268-3331
www.usps.com

Appendix III: GAO Contact and Staff Acknowledgments

GAO Contact	Lorelei St. James, (202) 512-2834 or stjamesl@gao.gov
Staff Acknowledgments	In addition to the contact named above, Teresa Anderson (Assistant Director), Amy Abramowitz, Shelby Kain, Margaret McDavid, SaraAnn Moessbauer, Amrita Sen, and Crystal Wesco made key contributions to this report.